10 TIPS

FOR

SELLERS

HOW NOT TO SCREW UP YOUR SALE AND SUCCESSFULLY GET TO THE CLOSING TABLE

ESSENTIAL INFORMATION YOU NEED TO KNOW

Carol Pro Murray

This fun, quick read is dedicated to Tom K. As my mentor and friend, I spent countless hours with him learning about the fascinating world of listing and selling homes. His influence was shared with my son, Charles, and after growing up in the business and obtaining his real estate license, he was fortunate to have Tom as a teacher also.

I am grateful for the education and all he imparted, as his knowledge of the subject was vast, and his execution was at times entertaining. RIP Tom, you are greatly missed by not only me but the real estate community as a whole.

Charles, I dedicate this book to you also. You've already experienced so much in so little time as a Realtor®. Your professionalism, dedication, commitment, and client-centered approach along with your charm and charisma have already made you an outstanding Realtor®.

The world is your oyster.

Table of Contents

Foreward

The ideas and insights in this book are gathered from my own experience of actively selling real estate. This is not a complete list of how not to screw up your home purchase, that would be impossible to guarantee. Weall go into "the process" with the best intentions. For the most part, with guidance from professionals, you'll be just fine.

Acknowledgement

Thank you to my many clients and cooperating agents throughout the years. Every transaction has taught me something different. You have all added to my bank of knowledge. Thank you also to my brokerage, Keller Williams Lakeside, its management, and all of the mentors who continue to impart their knowledge for us to continually grow and become better agents. And I would be remiss if I didn't acknowledge the great associates of NCI, School of Real Estate for their classes and continuing education every year.

CHAPTER 1

This Is Not Amateur Hour

You've decided to move - don't take it lightly! Moving can be a stressful experience, but with the right preparation and research, you can make this transition as smooth as possible. Don't worry, I'm here to help every step, well at least 10 of them, of the way. Start by assessing your needs and budget when deciding on a new home, and refer to my previously written book, 10 Tips for Homebuyers, How Not To Screw Up Your Purchase, And Successfully Get To The Closing Table.

Plan ahead and work with a licensed realtor. Make sure they have knowledge of the local market and listings. A good Realtor® will have communication skills, the ability to listen and understand what you need and be professional and responsible. Don't just choose some-one off of a list or internet search - take the time to get to know your agent so that you feel comfortable speaking openly with them. In the end, communication is key! The more communication between both parties, the smoother everything will go! In addition, choose an agent who will use a professional photographer for their photos, and possibly drone footage. This is not the amateur hour, the house must be shown in its best light, with the correct angles when potential buyers are looking at it online and making the decision as to whether or not to make an appointment. Trust me - you won't regret this decision! You can be sure that when it's all said and done you will have profited from one of your most valuable assets. A good Realtor® is worth their weight in gold! You can find a Realtor® in The National Association of Realtors, NAR directory.

CHAPTER 2
The Sad, Dead Plant

You know those half-done projects that you've put off for the last few years. Well, guess what time it is? It's time to repair and replace! Take care of any minor repairs or replacements around the house before listing it on the market. If potential buyers see projects that are half finished, they'll think that you haven't taken care of your home and will worry about the things they cannot see. Did you maintain the furnace? Did you clean out the gutters yearly? This list could go on and on.

Is it that difficult to put the closet door back on, or fix the track so buyers aren't looking directly into your abyss of clothing, if that truly is what you put in your closet? How about fixing the drywall where the toilet paper holder goes, and putting it back on? If you have young children, it probably has been knocked off the wall a time or two.

Furthermore, small updates like new faucets, knobs, and handles for your kitchen cabinetry or bathroom faucets can make an amazing difference in the look of your home without costing you much money at all! How about a new coat of paint? If you think you can't paint yourself or don't want to, check out some local painters through Nextdoor, or Facebook community groups. I'm not saying you have to or should repaint the whole house, even if it's just the entryway or front door, it makes a difference. If you have a finished basement, with ceiling tiles, please, please replace the ceiling tiles if they are water-stained, of course only after fixing the leak that could have happened yesterday or 3 years ago.

Curb appeal goes a long way in making buyers fall in love with your home. When I'm out touring homes, sometimes my buyers are standing right there on the front porch while I'm opening the lockbox, or while we're waiting for access. This gives them a few moments to mentally process what they see and that is their first impression! If the door paint is chipping, if the handle is rusted, or if there is trash sitting on the front porch or steps, this may be an immediate turn-off. In addition, if the plant that you placed on the porch looks sad, or is dead, please remove it. There's nothing worse than dead potted plants greeting potential buyers. Again, what else are you not taking care of?

Get rid of clutter and deep clean! This should probably go without saying, but I'm going to say it anyway. Make sure your home is clean and free of any odors. You want potential buyers to be able to picture themselves living in your space without any distractions. Clean up! Clutter is a big turnoff for buyers, so declutter and depersonalize the space to create an inviting atmosphere.

Clear off countertops, tables, and desks so they aren't cluttered with magazines, mail, and other items. If the front and/or sides of your refrigerator are full of pictures or the family calendar (like mine currently is), take them off. Put away the piles of laundry in the corner or on the steps and clear out anything you haven't used in a while. Clean up any pet hair or messes that may have been left behind - no one likes to see a dirty house! Be sure to also vacuum all carpets, rugs, and furniture, as well as mop the floors. Don't forget about windows either, make sure everything is squeaky clean so natural light can come in and make your home look brighter!

CHAPTER 3

Not Everyone Loves Animals As Much As You Do

If you have any pets, be sure to take them with you when buyers are viewing the house. They may be very cute, but not everyone loves animals as much as you do. You don't want buyers to be distracted by barking dogs or cats scratching furniture while they're trying to imagine themselves living in your home.

And of course, no one wants a smelly house, that's why it's also important to get rid of any odors before potential buyers view the house. Take out the trash regularly, freshen up carpets by using baking soda or an odor remover product, and open windows (weather permitting) when you have showings to let fresh air in.

Following these simple steps will ensure that potential buyers have a great first impression of your home and can focus on the positive aspects, rather than getting distracted by clutter or pet hair. So don't forget to take the time to DEEP. clean and de-clutter before you start showing your house! It'll be worth it when you get an offer from the perfect buyer.

It's also important to spruce up the exterior of your home too! Mow the lawn, edge sidewalks, and trim bushes/trees so buyers can see what kind of effort you put into caring for your property. A fresh layer of mulch will make your landscaping pop! A well-maintained front yard adds exponentially to your curb appeal. Don't forget to remove dead leaves left behind from the previous year that tend to accumulate in your landscape.

Ultimately, taking the time to thoroughly prepare your home before selling it is priceless - after all, you want the best return on investment possible! So make sure you give your house the TLC it needs to look its very best before putting it on the market. Don't let potential buyers be put off by disrepair, giving them a reason to lowball their offers. With a few easy tasks and some elbow grease, you can make sure your home is ready to attract the right buyer who will appreciate all of its wonderful features!

CHAPTER 4

Goldilocks and The Three Bears

Put away valuables. Brokers, Associate Brokers, and Salespersons cannot be responsible for any items that could potentially get stolen. Keep your most valuable and precious items out of sight in a secure location. This includes jewelry, documents, electronics, and anything else important to you before you start your showings. And if there is an heirloom light fixture or any other attached item that you may want to take with you when you move - replace it with something else before potential buyers come in.

Prospective buyers may come touring with their children or extended family. Even though it's their responsibility to watch the children, sometimes little ones see shiny items that draw their attention. Move anything that could be potentially dangerous. Furthermore, little ones have been known to try out beds (true story), like in Goldilocks and The Three Bears.

Don't price yourself out of the market. Most buyers will want to feel that they're getting a good deal, so be realistic and you can achieve that win-win! Your agent will research competitively priced homes in your area and make sure you're priced accordingly. Consider the size, location, and amenities of comparable homes when setting your asking price. Sellers can get ahead by doing their research and staying up to date on local market conditions so they know what buyers are looking for in a home. The more aware you are of current trends and pricing levels, the easier it is to competitively price your property and make sure it stands out from similar homes in your area.

This is what happens when your price yourself out of the market from the get-go: buyers will feel your home is overpriced, and they won't even go look at it. Then you'll have been on the market for a couple of weeks, and you may get upset with your agent who probably told you it was priced too high, to begin with. You'll begrudgingly agree to a small price drop, and then you may get a few more showings, but still won't receive any offers. Finally, you'll agree to price your home competitively, however, you won't be the new kid on the block anymore. Buyers may wonder what's wrong with your home and make the decision not to view it. So don't let this happen, find that sweet spot where buyers will line up to take a look and make an offer! That's the kind of outcome that all sellers are looking for. Be realistic and price your home correctly. It all starts with setting the right asking price, so get it right from the start.

CHAPTER 5
Silence is Golden and Loose Lips Sink Ships

Be flexible on showings, and make sure potential buyers have plenty of access to view the property. If you're only allowing showings on weekends or Tuesday nights, it won't help your effort to sell. Allow any day and time during the week that is convenient for agents and buyers so they can get a look at the property when they are ready. Also, if possible, leave while buyers view the house - that way they'll feel more comfortable. If you have to stay, go outside, in your car, or possibly in your garage. Disclaimer here- Don't sit in your car, that's in the garage, with it running, with the garage door shut! Just sayin'.

Silence is golden - stay out of the way and let potential buyers explore without feeling like they are being judged. If they have questions, their agent will be there to help them. You don't need to chime in, just be available for questions after the showing or when asked. Buyers want to feel like they can make the home their own, and will appreciate having the space to imagine what their furnishings would look like in the different rooms. Let me add something here also, much of the public has security cameras installed in their homes. If you're a seller that does, and you can see and hear what's happening at the showing, as in the buyers discussing, or in some cases, stating what they don't like about the home, try not to let it affect you. Remember, you have to emotionally detach from the sale. Try not to let your ego get involved. Remember the reason you listed- to sell!

Let me reiterate because this is so important, loose lips sink ships, let buyers view and make decisions on their own, without unsolicited input from you. Allowing them this freedom will help create an atmosphere of trust and confidence between both parties and increase the chances of a successful sale.

CHAPTER 6
Bigger, Better Offers

Act fast on offers - don't sit on them for days, you'll risk buyers feeling unimportant and walking away from a potential sale. Counter the offer if you're not happy with it, but don't let your ego (here it is again) get in the way. Countering can help bridge a gap to reach a win-win situation, so make sure to negotiate at least within reason and give buyers something they're willing to work with. But be warned, don't hold an offer waiting for a better one. It may never come. The best bet if you're not happy with the offer is to counter it. That way there's still hope of coming to an agreement that both sides will be content with! At this point, communication and openness are key. Your agent and the buyer's agent will make sure both parties are aware of deadlines and expectations during negotiations. Again, you don't want your ego clouding your judgment.

If by chance you are fortunate to have multiple offers your agent can call a "highest and best", which is alerting all the agents to have their buyer clients bring their best offer, financially, and in terms, to the table. This is beneficial for you, the seller, as it gives an opportunity for an increased sale amount for your home and may also include favorable terms, like occupancy after closing, closing costs paid by buyers, and/or other contingencies a buyer will waive to make their offer stand out. Again, be prepared to act quickly when presented with multiple offers - these don't come around often and can be a great opportunity for sellers if handled correctly!

Don't always assume a cash offer is the best, VA Loans and Conventional Loans can be just as beneficial. Your agent will explain the differences in offers and ultimately which one would be the best fit for you. In regards to terms, maybe you're looking at taking an offer that will give you free occupancy, or one that will close sooner than later. Or, one that may waive an inspection contingency.

One of the most important documents in the offer I believe is the loan pre-approval or pre-qualification letter. It is imperative to have your agent call the lender to verify the ability of the buyer to purchase the home. This step is crucial and should not be skipped - make sure you are working with a qualified buyer who can provide that they are capable of buying your home! A pre-approval letter shows their commitment and willingness, so this will go a long way in helping close the deal. Additionally, sometimes lenders will call your agent on behalf of their buyer, this is usually a sign of a lender who's committed to getting the sale to the closing table.

CHAPTER 7
Due Diligence

Once an offer is made, be aware that if you aren't happy with it and decide to counter it, the original offer becomes null and void. The buyer can walk away, that's why it's important to think about your counter seriously. Again, don't let your ego get in the way. Both parties are looking for the same outcome, it's a matter of at what price and terms. Try not to come back with an insulting amount, even if they insulted you with theirs. Remember, agents must present all offers to their sellers, as ridiculous as they may be. We are there to provide advice, advocacy, and negotiation skills as your Realtor®.

If all parties come to a "meeting of the minds", it's time to execute the purchase agreement. Executing the agreement is when both parties come together and sign on the line. Executing the purchase agreement also creates a binding contract between both parties that outlines expectations and rules for each party going forward until closing. It's important to read through everything thoroughly before signing - if there are contingencies then your agent will walk you through them in more detail. As a licensed Realtor® I strongly suggest if you have any concerns about the contract, please have an attorney review it prior to signing it.

Executing the agreement isn't the end of the process, there are still a few steps before closing! Both parties will need to complete their due diligence, which means buyers may conduct a home inspection (paid for by the buyer), an appraisal may be ordered, and any necessary updated loan documents will be gathered for your buyer's lender. During this time both parties need to remain open-minded and negotiate in good faith. If something during the inspection is found unsatisfactory to the buyers, then be prepared to address it. More than likely the buyer will ask you to remedy the issue or will ask for a financial reduction in the price or a credit at the closing. No matter what happens though, keep your cool. Emotions do run high during this time and harsh words can make the sale fall apart. Calm communication is key when dealing with unexpected issues during due diligence!

CHAPTER 8
Read, Understand, and Read Again

Now the underwriting process begins for your buyer. This is when lenders review the borrower's loan application and all the necessary documents to see if they meet (still qualify) the underwriting guidelines. The underwriting process can take days or a few weeks. Buyers may have conditions they need to clear. At this point, your buyer may need to update docs (bank statements, pay stubs, etc.) for their lender, depending on when they received their pre-approval or pre-qualification letter. Some lenders have their buyers "all set" and the only item that is needed is the appraisal. In addition, depending on how much your buyer is putting down, the lender may waive the appraisal. Of course, if your buyer is purchasing with cash, the appraisal is not mandatory, only needed if it is a request by your buyer and included on the purchase agreement. In most cases, the buyer is paying for their appraisal. There are times when an appraisal comes in lower than the purchase price. Depending on the circumstances of the loan, there may need to be additional negotiation. This is one reason why it is so important to read and understand your purchase agreement. Remember, your contract can have legally binding verbiage, and as such another reason I recommend using a licensed Realtor® for your home sale.

After underwriting is complete, buyers may still need additional time to secure their funds and/or address any conditions of the approval. Once all conditions are met and a clear to close has been given, it's finally time to set a closing date! Your agent will work with the buyer's agent and title company to schedule a suitable closing date that works for everyone involved. It's important to stay informed of any last-minute changes or documents needed before closing to avoid any delays.

CHAPTER 9
No One Likes Shady

In most cases, buyers request a final walk-through before closing and during this time they will inspect all items agreed upon in the purchase agreement. This is their final chance to ensure that the home is in the same condition it was when initially seen. If you, as a seller has had any mechanical issues; furnace, hot water tank, air conditioning, water leaks, or other issues please tell your agent so they can advise you. No one likes these kinds of surprises. It's your responsibility, as you are the owner of the home, to get whatever is not working fixed before closing. This is usually made clear on the purchase agreement you signed. Be prepared to attend to any issues with the buyers if they're unhappy with the walk-through. Keep in mind most agents prepare their buyer clients that the home should be kept in approximately the same condition, and "broom swept" clean when vacated by the seller. If your buyer is not happy with the condition of the home make sure to address it immediately. Your agent will communicate with your buyer's agent to come to a resolution that pleases both parties. Remember, your buyer still has not signed on the dotted line. You don't want to come this far to "throw the baby out with the bath water". Of course, this is just an old saying, and like the saying, you'd never throw the baby out, therefore you shouldn't "throw" the entire deal away, you've come too close to finalizing the deal.

Don't be too concerned about the walk-through. If you've been upfront with your agent/buyers then you have nothing to worry about. Honesty is the best and only policy. You could possibly open yourself up to legal ramifications if you attempt to be shady. Don't be shady.

CHAPTER 10
Don't Forget Your ID

Once everything has been finalized and the buyers have conducted their walk-through, it's finally time for the closing! At closing, both parties sign all documents needed to transfer the property. The title company will be responsible for disbursing funds and ensuring all paperwork is properly filed with the appropriate agencies to make sure the process goes smoothly. Here are some key things to remember, make sure everyone arrives with a valid ID. Without proper identification, your closing may be delayed. If the buyer is getting the keys at closing, be sure to remember the garage door remotes, extra keys, and keypad information, if needed. Lastly, don't forget to transfer your utilities out of your name as of the end of the day of closing. Do not have the utilities SHUT OFF. Utility companies are famous for turning off the electricity and gas before the buyer has had a chance to put them in their name. Again, your agent should remind you of this final step, as well as the buyer's agent informing the buyer to put the utilities in their name.

Closing is an exciting process for both parties involved. It's a culmination of hard work and dedication from everyone participating to make sure everything goes off without a hitch. With good communication and understanding between buyers and sellers, the closing day will be a breeze! As long as you have been honest about all disclosures and everything has gone according to plan then you should have nothing to worry about at closing. Happy Closing Day!

Conclusion

Listing your home for sale can be an overwhelming experience. This should be an enjoyable and exciting time - make the most of it! Enjoy the process and the memories that may come along with it. Sometimes setbacks may occur, don't get discouraged, pivot if needed, and continue on. Remember, since you're selling your home, try to look at it without an emotional attachment. It's difficult, but know you're only leaving the physical space, and you'll carry whatever memories you want with you onto the next place. With a bit of hard work, you will be able to move on to your next chapter in no time. Best of luck!

Bonus Material

Make sure to get a head start when it comes to packing up your home before listing - the less clutter around, the more your house will "show" its best features. Pack away personal items like photos, knick-knacks, and other decorations you might be attached to! Plus, if you've already started packing before an offer is accepted, it makes moving day that much easier. Don't forget: even with all the planning in the world, Murphy's Law can still come into play - so make sure you have a good Realtor® backing you up with sound advice!

Afterword

I strongly suggest a future or repeat home-seller work with a Real Estate Professional when looking to sell a home. If you'd like any additional information, or would like a referral for a vetted, listing or selling agent in your area, please don't hesitate to reach out to myself or my colleague, Charles Provenzano, of The Proven Property Team, at Keller Williams Lakeside Market Center, Shelby Township, Michigan.

https://carolpro.kw.com/

carolpro@kwlakeside.com

586-685-1250